Bilingual Press/Editorial Bilingüe

General Editor
   Gary D. Keller

Managing Editor
   Karen S. Van Hooft

Associate Editors
   Barbara H. Firoozye
   Thea S. Kuticka

Assistant Editor
   Linda St. George Thurston

Editorial Board
   Juan Goytisolo
   Francisco Jiménez
   Eduardo Rivera
   Mario Vargas Llosa

Address:
   Bilingual Press
   Hispanic Research Center
   Arizona State University
   P.O. Box 872702
   Tempe, Arizona 85287-2702
   (480) 965-3867

red

Alfred Arteaga

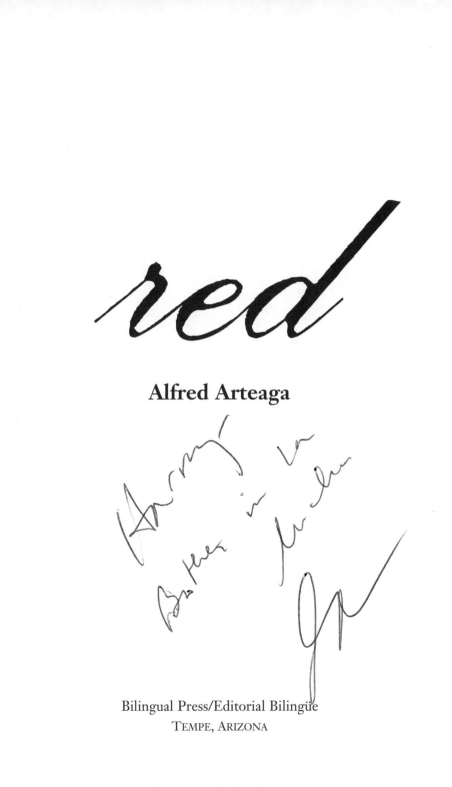

Bilingual Press/Editorial Bilingüe
TEMPE, ARIZONA

ISBN 0-927534-94-0

Library of Congress Cataloging-in-Publication Data

Arteaga, Alfred, 1950-
   Red / Alfred Arteaga.
     p. cm.
   Poems in English or Spanish.
   ISBN 0-927534-94-0 (alk. paper)
     I. Title.

PS3551.R726 R43 2000
811'.54—dc21   00-039765

PRINTED IN THE UNITED STATES OF AMERICA

Cover design by Sercan Sahin
Back cover photo © 2000, Tisa Reeves

Para Mireya
hija mía

Other Works by Alfred Arteaga

POETRY
Cantos
Love in the Time of Aftershocks

CREATIVE NONFICTION
House with the Blue Bed

THEORY
Chicano Poetics
An Other Tongue

Contents

Diversos

Cartas

Silvas Humanas

Love in the Time of Aftershocks

Nunca nadie me podrá parar
Sólo muerto me podrán callar

—CAIFANES

Diversos

TENTLI

Tentli -s. labio; pico de ave; hocico de animal; orilla de
algo; fig. memoria, recuerdo, tira de escritura.

Think of the mouth as port of desire,
an edge that marks thought from
sky and the flight of birds. Want across
dreams recalled days after, desire itself
written like past motion in light.
Lip is edge, the border demarking in light
and in light of day, desire is that edge,
that border, trim and light. Had we but
edge equal to desire, bound by our simple
plans and steps of desire. Bound by our
binds of brave blows, destruction for
certain, mouth of such desire, mouth
of sex and the sex of sex, had we but
the motion at edge to take bright
time, brave motion, and destroy
some center in its cool repose.

DRIVING IN FOG

She breaks silent, "Asina
es perder el alma," gives voice
once. This is how it feels, driving
in fog. What time is it after all
to lose one's soul may be what
she felt but just asked, "¿Qué
horas son?" What if you run off
into the fog and I never see you
again, even as I stop and peer? What
if I want so much to touch your skin?
If the sound of heavy wind is all
we'll ever hear, if there is nothing
beyond an edge, just beyond
our sight? Does it creep into the car
interior, so diffuse up close I don't
see it fog the windshield with its
thinnest of membranes?
The point about fog is that this
muffled obfuscation is swirling, top
quarks of fog set loose, decaying, and
it matters not whether we know this,
fog is now only and will never be.
Whether gift, blessing or sign: it is fog.
It is not as the Russians believe,
not like flying diaphanous in deep air.
I am driving in fog. Where are you beside

BLOOD, SAND, BLOOD

for kyf

A perfect walk up from the water
round Mullaghmore, the little boats
becoming more so, shrink
in view then wait in memory
behind the hill. Tomorrow Bundoran
or Lissadell, it makes such little difference,
we'll walk about the same, and this
bright light can neither repeat nor fade.
Though pleasure craft may diminish and finally
sink from view, though I sweat, you slow,
we are the distant sinking's fiery glow.

Amor y caos

Antes, el día antes, había las cosas,
horas de cosas, reglas y máquinas.
Nací, lo sé por la lógica griega y
por el orden de la historia del hombre.
Antes, el día antes, tuve yo una vida,
debe ser, y tuve momentos, llamas
verdes, azules, y una fe, tuve fe.
¿Por qué los libros, las fotos y huellas,
sino pruebas del diccionario, sino
del paso perdido de cristo, sino
la línea quebrada que llega hasta ti?
Se dice que antes existían cosas,
la muralla de minutos, fil de horas;
un sueño lleno, dicen mis amigos,
existía antes de que te conocí.
Antes no había nada.
En tus ojos no nací aquel momento
ni en tu vista comenzó mi vida allá,
pero después, un día después, cayó
el pasado a pedazos, a pedazos.
No dudo ni creo yo:
Antes, el día antes, había las cosas,
y antes no había nada.
En tu vista verde de caos ando,
en tu respiro mi paso de nuevo,
en tus dedos de minutos el tiempo.
Quebrado al momento ando,
suelto de la significación, la ley,
aquí en el detalle claro de tu ser.

7/15/95 París

Camino imaginado

Blue leaves, hojas rotas in the shape of stars.
Ni un "no" en tu vocabulario but for others;
blue in place of green in the shape of Spain.
Ojos the color of dirt, chocolate, coffee, time,
azules las horas, hojas de horas van y se van,
ni una palabra, ni una queja, nor broken bit
a tu lado beside me andamos walking, sí walking
caminamos caminos like these, such streets, what
city.

7/15/95 Paris

Amor, Reading Letters

En el pequeño mundo de las letras
lo posible se acuesta con la física.
Por ejemplo: fueron hojas azules
que quité de tu cabello anoche,
las mismas que hallamos en los planos
impresos del museo d'Orsay,
las cuales recogí de tu jardín.
Por eso me enamoré contigo,
ladrillo a ladrillo, beso a mirada,
muralla, beso, pájaro, pluma.
Me llamas Ulises, y regreso, regresado,
mientras tu lees o tejes o fijas.

I imagine in truth because some things I know
so well: that she reads before she sleeps, shakes
her head, dives back to the sea.

8/8/95 Berkeley

BC

UN DIÁLOGO POR AUSENTES

Not as she is, but as she fills his dreams.
—Christina Rossetti

CRISTÓBAL ROSALES, EL ACUARELISTA,
PENSANDO EN LA AUSENCIA, ESTUDIA LA
MANO EN LA LUZ GRIS DE LA TARDE.
La traza colorida
que me engaña ya
que has huido, florece
este lado del aliento,
fuera, en el pleno aire
del sometimiento
en la cuna del tacto.

BEATRIZ ESPINOSA DESPIERTA MÁS
TEMPRANO EN UNA MAÑANA SIN COLOR.
Un día como los demás
el mismo sol calienta los ojos
y una vez más, colores y líneas comienzan a acoplar;
bestias, selvas y unas calles curiosas,
como si pudieran, me preguntarían
¿por qué no te ausentas, para qué sirve el horizonte?
Examino el músculo, el hueso y
la piel en que consistes, tú que estiras en
la mañana, pálido, la mañana descolorida.

Con lápiz y pincel, hazme
en cuadro plano, suelta mi perfil
de tu paleta y enciérrame en
acuarelas claras y frías, frías
como tu brazo, como tu respiro,
al último momento antes
de despertar, cuerpo
frío.

Los dibujos significan nada,
alivian ningún dolor, gastan
el tiempo, la perspectiva
y la visión.
No nunca más te despertaré.
Quédate aquí inmóvil, atrás, pintado
por tu maña triste.

Fuera de esta casa, de este taller de cuadros,
hay un charco que veo y que estuve mirando.
Es un cuerpo de agua, se aguanta entre
zoquete y cielo. Más profundo debe estar
al medio. Me voy. Tocaré la mera orilla
fría pero transparente.

EL ACUARELISTA PONE LA MANO ENFRENTE
DEL ROSTRO Y HABLA.
Beso colorado,
pintado aquí en la mano persistes;
qué vida el color rosa
y la rosa figura
te dan.

Writing Verse in Berkeley

First, examine your hand
for just hand
draws mind to paper.
The hand is not body, not noun, an act
like spark: kinesis,
electric.

Next, watch for one day
the hand act a full 24 hours, sleep even.
Note each pause, sign of weakness,
and every excess of force, no
matter how slight.
Record its casual and reflexive
grasp as well as the objects it grasps.
Schematize its movements into
a style of movement and conclude
in the act, and this is most important—
know in the act—that push
subjects things to verse: the index
of motivation, the wave of palm,
the nail tears and scratch.

Only then, fill
hand like glove, do what you will.
By sheer will power, make
hand make verse.

Afterwords, among the poets,
keep it still: neither act nor write,
freeze hand, torso and leg.
Do not tap the floor
even absently. Yet keep the eye free,
keep free the ear, the mouth.
Clearly hear Cynthia pierce one line,
"the irony . . ." focus
on the metal *in her voice* that
can rust, can be magnetized.
For this is what is
in verse: words rust, words magnetize:
attract, repel, decay.
Recall a trick of children:

> *Four dark coins touch in line*
> *on a smooth light surface. Press down*
> *three with three fingers of your hand.*
> *Push a new coin, hit the rest,*
> *and break the last coin free.*

It can never matter how hard, nor even if, you press,
it will always fly beyond your reach.

TOMORROW TODAY

OCTOBER 11, 1995

Tomorrow marks
five hundred and three years
since Columbus found his way
to the Americas, half
a millennium and three years
since the story of contact began,
since Europe came west.
Tomorrow marks the anniversary.
Five hundred and three winters
have transpired, as many springs,
summers, and falls. Those seasons
are gone, those times have passed,
there is nothing we can do,
they are gone.
Tomorrow we will remember
October 12th, 1492,
here in the United States,
tomorrow will be Columbus Day;
here in Berkeley,
it will be Indigenous Peoples' Day;
here in Califas, Aztlán,
it will be Día de la Raza.
As many winters have passed,
as many suns have set, as many
minutes and seconds have come
and gone, up to the same tomorrow:
Columbus Day, Indigenous Peoples' Day,

Día de la Raza;
but they are not the same.
For we are different and we mean different
when we celebrate
the discovery of a new world, imagine,
a new world, or different when we solemnize
the most severe genocide in the history
of the world, the most severe, or when
we recognize the birth of a new race,
a new race. For twenty-four hours tomorrow
we can celebrate the greatest act
of the Renaissance and the act of a single man
in Columbus Day,
and we can solemnize
the deaths of tens of millions
of Native Americans and the extermination
of whole peoples, such as those
on the islands of first contact,
remembered in Indigenous Peoples' Day
and we can
recognize miscegenation and the possibility
of contact between races
in the birth of hybrid, mestizo peoples
in the Día de la Raza.
Tomorrow is Columbus Day,
it is Indigenous Peoples' Day,
it is Día de la Raza: all exactly
mark five hundred and three years
and all exactly mark something different.
The events that have happened
in the interim have happened,
nothing can change that.
The first joy at the sight of land

happened. The unspeakable terror
of parents watching their child
fed to conquistadors' dogs happened.
Five hundred and three years of events
took place, we cannot change that.
We cannot stand up like Las Casas
and say this must stop; we cannot
tell the Tainos, on first seeing the Spanish arrive,
to run, to run, and not to stop running.
What was, was.
We cannot change the number of days, nor
can we change the events that happened.
We can, though, choose to remember or forget,
to celebrate, solemnize, recognize.

Last year
my state expressed hatred for my people,
marking in law Mexicans as the common evil,
going as far as denying vaccine
so that those of us not deported, aborted,
or incarcerated, could die from childhood disease.
The majority of Anglo Americans, of African Americans,
Asian Americans, the majority of women
supported proposition 187.
Why?
Why is it that Chicanos and some Latinos
are the only people whose majority opposed it?
I am not bitter, but I do not forgive.
Don't all of us know, don't we all realize,
the terrible danger when we allow ourselves
to choose among ourselves and choose one
people for exclusion? Don't we realize
what we do to ourselves when we delude

ourselves and support a solution that marks
one people illegal? Any ultimate solution,
any ethnic cleansing, any racism,
any xenophobia of hate, hurts us all.
Each and every one.
For each small act of exclusion
opens the door for more.

This year,
the regents denied affirmative action.
Those regents who direct the university
that employs me, that educated me,
voted for exclusion.
This year, they met and they voted
to prevent Cal and UCLA,
to prevent Riverside, Irvine, and San Diego,
Santa Cruz, Santa Barbara,
Davis, and San Francisco, to prevent
this university from fair policy,
from policy that opposes the practice of exclusion,
from policy that has made opportunities
for people, including me.
Earlier this year the regents so voted.

Tomorrow, we will not be able to change
five hundred and three years of events:
Columbus did what Columbus did; whole
peoples have been exterminated, nothing can
bring them back. But tomorrow, we can
choose to remember or forget, and if to
remember, we can choose how to recall,
we can decide what all that time, all those events,
what all those acts mean.

And our act is significant.
It is true that the regents have voted,
it is true that they have struck down
affirmative action, but it is not true
that nothing can be done about it:
the matter is not over.
Each regent who voted is still alive
and more importantly, I am alive,
and more importantly still, we
are gathered tonight here and we
say the matter is not over.
Some things cannot be changed
but this can.
Whether any individual regent
voted out of intimidation by the governor,
or to support his presidential bid,
whether out of deep seated racism, or
naive misconception: it does not matter:
that vote was wrong.
I stand here now and say to you
it is wrong to impede us; any step backward
hurts us all. Those who imagine good
from a politics of exclusion delude
themselves: each selfish gain comes at
a cost to all: we share the university,
we share the state.
Affirmative action is not dead history,
sealed and written, it is a live issue
one that right now we are waging.
I stand opposed to racism,
opposed to sexism,
opposed to ethnocentrism.
I oppose the politics of exclusion.
I affirm our action.

Lebensraum

Das Gringo Volk braucht Lebensraum
for theirs is the greed of greed.
The gringo folk need living space
to bury, to bank, to breathe.
Al gringo le falta más room to live
que la avarcia puede ganar,
ciento ochenta y siete grados más
que la avaricia propia puede agarrar.
The gringo folk need more dead space
free from natives, their kids, their words,
a living space above the dead,
to capitalize on greed of greed.
Das Gringo Volk braucht Lebensraum
dead space that makes no sense,
200 million dollars saved for billions lost
to deny Mexican kids vaccine
and a place to write, to read.
The greed of greed is the law of the land
in Kalifornia, Kapital of the dead.

Prayer for the Death of the Soul

We pray for death of one soul.
One man, who may in his heart have love
for others, love for other men, for women, children.
We do not see his love and do not know
nor can know what is in his heart,
for that is known to you alone.
But his mind's work we see.
He has taken his wisdom, and bent by hate,
he has come to hate. He has come to hate
the rainbow you gave us, proof of your undying love,
and he strikes at our eyes.
His mind, so torn by fear, has come to fear
the sounds of our names, our voices,
and he strikes at our ears and tongues.
And what he does to us, he does to himself.
He claws his own skin at night and when he is alone,
he cries out because he has cut
to his very soul and killed the gift you gave.
We pray for the soul he has killed.
Deliver him from himself.
And deliver us from such hate and fear.

Net Laguna

Je voudrais dormir au bord du lac,
al lado de este que en inglés es lack,
to sleep beside lo que je voudrais,
junto al lago peut-être nager.

Je voudrais dormir in the wide aire
mentir in the cut, herida mía;
avoir des rêves al revés de anger,
rage, où nagent les anges d'argent,
rien, and rain entero peace of time.

To ask la cuna of first, ¿qué es, pez?
Passé pescado, sin essense, pecado original,
con d'ailleurs de l'essence un seul poisson,
the poison sol au bord laguna cut water
corps de l'eau, de l'heure, and the fold que eres.

Une tranche de la vie, flesh bits, minutiæ,
¿qu'a bu qui a vu qué ha visto l'año que entra quién?

Blue, Sharp, Still

is not water
or ways emptied
of dust broken black.
Curved fact of thing nothing like
sub-things and para-thing

Not at this moment, pretend at this, of gazure beneath and
amid the broken stream of inanimates thriving across broad
bands, not what is then agreed to as the full impression of
things, pretend, the impression of matter on things that
issue. Palettes before the black surface of things-in-fact
shine if they could or could not lie before the issue of
breakage confronting spill invented as some thing scene:

Therefore the emotion
thus rendered tangible
is by the sense of break
a whole black palette
imagined lucid
as so the start off perch
is the narrowed band
and length
and this short length
is trace only
and this sense is
that of short length
unlike another or the
midnight fire of any
para-thing's heat

and is the convergence
of angles narrowed
length and depth
and wide too terminal.
This thing of unreflected
surface and effulgent core
gives back the whole white
in silver bands of if
it had volition unchecked
or broken like the arc
is broken water.

The convergence is one that facts potential of energy in
form, relying, pretend, on the real of consistency and the
is of shape to incise and cleave like it does. The point of
issue is its relentless, pretend, push to self, expressing in
potential the plunge and thrust and narrow angle of a
matter on the verge of break, the slender break, unlike
the spill but near time

Cartas

ESCRITO EN AGUA

Se acaban los seis años de sequía
fácilmente: dedos de agua llegan
por fin a la cara seca, la cara retirada.
La casa, la camisa,
traspasada por lluvia demasiado
atenta, se convierten en líneas
de versos de bestias de selvas de hojas de papel
secas, mojadas, remojadas.
Por seis años una California sin
canto, sin ganas existía. El color de aire,
agua es algo común. Se dicen
que no existe en el desierto,
pero fíjate: hay bastante en sombra y letra
para creer en vida por toda la vida y además
para terminar una época seca, para matar
silencio en las hojas.

12.3.93

TROZOS

Si *pedazo* no tiene una esencia propia
y, a la vez, es la pura verdad que
nunca alcanzaremos un cuerpo móvil
que ya ha arrancado ayer,
¿cómo podemos comunicar? A pedazos
llegaremos, tantas aguas diáfanas, cuando
la luz reteblanca se quiebra encima de
la mesa y revela a sí mismo
esencialmente: lo que es una gota a otra, es
tal trozo humano a tal fragmento
nocturnal de la ciudad, es isla
a la marea menguante:
pasos claros, ocultos, atraviesan el mar
lago, laguna, lágrima, huellas
en las pieles de un agua quebradiza,
fronteriza, traspasada no más con un cambio
de ser, una pausa al medio corriente,
hasta bruma, vapor, o humedad necia.
Claro, se trasluce y se vierte en seguida,
el blanco pedazo del sagrado blanco,
y sin esencia, enajenan todos los
fragmentos, insensibles.
¿Qué hay? ¿Qué cae?

Varias respuestas

La música, por ejemplo,
existe al momento.
Su recuerdo nos engaña
precisamente porque es
mentira. El dibujo que miras
después de cerrar los ojos
no se distingue mucho
de cualquier foto o pintura: es
algo visto, es algún ser. Lo que
puedes detener, parar en media
vuelta, es algo, claro, pero no es
vuelta, ni corriente, ni ritmo.
La vida, por ejemplo, cruza
líneas y nos desengaña
aunque creemos el contrario:
no es cosa, ni tiene ser.
Los versos se despiden así,
acuérdate. Los huesos se despiden
así. Tantos ecos, así.

24.4.93

La joda española

Si por muerte entendemos el sereno
y por vida entendemos lo sereno . . .
      No.
Si está lleno el autobús de desconocidos
hasta dormidos unos
pero sé bien de dónde vengo y más o menos
a qué hora acabaré . . .
      Mejor.
Cuando te veo de paso me pongo a dormir,
si por paso entendemos el tráfico ilegal
y por "tú" y "yo" entendimos la misma cosa . . .
      Sí.
Largos están los caminos reales hasta la muerte
y qué pena dar una mala vuelta: a los lados, afilado,
no es hielo, es vidrio, es espejo, es nada.

Palabras masculinas

Mentira pura la letra,
la desesperanza, la fortaleza:
mentira pura el dios inhábil
de las tres cruces, tres veces
desocupado: mentira las nubes
que mienten y que se hacen
tales ficciones: y más mentira
el amor que arde hasta el hueso,
irradiando lo que no puede quemar.
Pura mentira pura la pureza de la
mentira más mentida. No es que no más
no creo en las letras: no
creo que existen: aquí sólo yo grito
solamente en la plena luna
"mentira". Por eso vale el sexo:
sí puede mentir pero, ¿para qué?
Si es o no es, no me importa,
lo que vale no cuenta.

19.9.93

Aparte ir

Después de la muerte del tono,
queja de la línea telefónica,
persiste el recado, son y paso
de la estructura del danzón: estampillas
despegadas con cartas blancas: qué
selvas matinales, maritales, qué danza
marginal, qué pelo negro. Así
desenmarañan nuestras piernas así,
tuya, mía, mía, tuya:
la trenza que un día nos hicimos
desenreda, y el doble hélice
que enlaza a ti y el que enlaza a mí,
día con día, también: tal como
pierna y pelo, el ADN. Aparte
te vas, me voy: la distancia
en los matorrales.

Rama

No hay versos en los árboles,
      pero sí hay papeles.
No hay aduanas en los romances,
      pero hay pistolas.
No hay nada que tomar en el hospital,
      no más hay tiempo.
No hay bastantes horas,
      sólo rinde el cambio.
No hay nada más que tristes monedas en la iglesia,
      mas el crucifijo.
No se halla cura en un perdido veneno,
      porque las aguas de reflexión ocupan espacio:

Cae la catedral y sube el agua a la vez
      a causa del reflejo y el ser de la superficie del lago,
      y refluyen más allá de los orígenes ocultos,
      olvidados o perdidos.

18.4.94

COORDINADA

Después del abandono, traición,
desprecio, rechazo, huida, fastidio, [fatiga]
amor obsesionante, amor puro, mero y honrado,
muerte de un hijo, primer beso, carta tarde,
y el perder todo menos a ella,
permanece lo más pobre que nos da la ciencia.
Las coordinadas cartesianas localizan
cualquier cuerpo humano en el espacio:
equis, i griega y a veces, la zeta,
explican todo y nos ofrecen el consuelo
racional, que quiere decir, lo desapasionado.
Pero como llegamos a experimentar:
el cambio cambia a uno y a los dos,
el sujeto no es igual a, ni se refiere
a, su pobre yo. Nunca en ninguna vida.
El cuerpo tal como el alma no es número,
ni es el rumbo de la vida una ecuación linear.
Sólo dejamos con la probabilidad
y la estadística: ella esta aquí, casi, quizás,
ahorita, parece. Y la coordinada nada vale.

9.5.94

CUENTOS IMPASIBLES

1 luna para ti.
2 soles para que te ardes para mí.
3 dedos desmochados para ti.
4 papeles blancos para mí.
5 iglesias de cartón.
6, para mí, vasos vacíos de verdad.
7 cosas perdidas, como la sombra anoche.
8 veces solo.
9 corazones de piedras verdes para ti.
10 veces tarde para mí.
11 es nada y tú lo guardas bien.
2 soles para que te ardes para mí.

7.6.94

La red

Una matriz es el abecedario,
o, por lo menos, una serie estrellada,
una actriz desafortunada, acostumbrada
a dormir sola. Me desmiente en
media locución con su mudo perder:
cae abrazo a un acto desanimado, a pedazos,
lo que fuera el acto del brazo
cae a una significación, una avaricia
del deseo sin conexión al querer.
La telenovela conecta las quejas
de Hollywood o Churrubusco
a mi genio raso, estrellado ya.
Y la ausencia del caso no es una treta
temporal, pero acaso la red se anima
el fin de los ángeles. Y en fin me quedo
preguntando, ¿por qué es femenina
la mano, es masculino el dedo, y femenina
la uña? ¿Y por qué tropiezo tanto,
sin sueño con la red?

13.7.94

Contrabando y natación

Pero, al acabar de desear,
¿cuáles aguas imaginadas?
Labios son libros en algún sentido.
Como impregnan las hojas y
se derraman las letras hasta
la significación, y eso aunque
se localizan lejos del borde de
los lagos del significado.
La mano sentida, dormida
la izquierda, frías las dos,
tratan de nadar como árboles
californios, como las manzanitas,
por ejemplo, en medio de una
niebla de comprender. Sí,
sí hay el trabajo de la boca, sí,
la pureza del tráfico nos emociona, y sí,
la encrucijada también.

Silvas Humanas

AMOR

Usted se halla en la ciudad
nueva, yendo por el metro, no, mejor
afuera, viajando en un tren, dejando
atrás y a la mano derecha cualquier
edificio o rascacielos inútil
a través de la ventana borrosa,
montaje y borrador, allí esperando
adelante, en tal trayecto tal hora,
el próximo pueblo, por lo cual busca
para descubrir lo que proponen el
mundo, el tren, los sentidos humanos.
Porque aquí la luz traspasa el vidrio en
planos geométricos, se da cuenta
de las naturalidades de Juan Gris
por primera vez, planos claros de un sol
ardiente más allá de la ventana
cerrada, claros planos ya adentro en el
coche del tren, banderas luminosas,
como si la luz tuviera sustancia
ondeante, navajas brillantes, como
si diera a luz la luz a un corazón que
recordaría este sueño de dormir
sólo al despertar. La luz que revela
al mundo afuera, el árbol, automóvil,
la niña jugando lejos, divulga
también, y con la misma facilidad,
las cosas del mundo dentro del coche,
en este lado del vidrio, tan fácil,
aunque es más chico el mundo móvil, mundo
hecho partículas, más frío a causa

de las leyes de física que tratan
de tamaño y temperatura óptima.
Un plano de luz tienta
la cara de ella de repente como
antagonista a ella sola, porque
para los otros pasajeros aquí en
el mundo chico, móvil, apartados,
ellos con sombreros, que fijan libro
y periódico, que hablan un poco,
fuman poco, para cada uno de ellos
la luz es cosa distinta pero no el
plano fatal de una tragedia griega
manifestado en onda y partícula
en seguida, tirado por la diosa
envidiosa, feroz, exactamente
a la piel, al labio, al ojo de esta
cara distinta a los cien kilómetros
por hora ahora. Pero ¿quien va a ganar,
las fuerzas naturales, que se acercan
muy cerca a la fuerza del destino, o la
cara de una mujer que es tan humana?
Pone abajo, a su lado, en el asiento
vacío, el libro adornado con letras
y colores interesantes, y en un
movimiento gracioso se levanta
de intento y al principio comienza con la
mano izquierda, luego con las dos, jala
el visillo y vislumbra la sombra aquí en
el mundo de los sentados móviles.
Por unos kilómetros
usted se ha dado cuenta que ese libro
ruso de escritora armenia ha cambiado,
casi como si una voz incógnita

articulara la palabra impresa
y la hoja encuadernada al momento de
la lectura y el toque del libro ruso, o en
otro sentido, como si se hubiera
convertido en una de esas pinturas
cubistas de dicho libro, un ejemplar
de tal europa, porque claro que sí
es Europa, fantástica por causa
de ser una sin muerte. Pero no es, es
el baile de luz y sombras, el viaje
de Dante hasta el infierno por segunda
clase, viaje a la nación del destino
se dice en el boleto, la hora, origen
y destino, el precio: luz y sombras más
y más pesadas, el ritmo más y más
lento, una música que se oye por la
primera vez, danza típica y triste
despacio van los pasos indígenas
despacio, pasos quietos, despacio más.
Alzo la pluma, cierro el
cuaderno para más fácilmente entrar
al mundo vivo y ambulante en que me hallo
también y además, para contemplar los
planos claros e invisibles de una luz
colorida en su quietud elemental
aquí en medio del mismo viaje, otro
pasajero con su reloj e imagen
de la red de paradas blanco y negro.
A ella digo pocas palabras porque
aunque falla fácilmente la lengua
y se confunden los sentidos, es más
complicado cuando ella piensa en la
tragedia griega clásica mientras lee

una novela rusa, en una rusa
armiñada, por eso digo unas
pocas palabras en un castellano
americano, el mismo que hablaría
con catalán o filipino. Pero
porque se trata de amor, yo toco la
cara de ella con los mismos dedos
con que yo detengo la pluma, pero
sin pensar en escribir, tocar hasta
ver la diferencia en temperatura
de cuerpo a cuerpo, la que significa,
según la famosa psicoanalista
francesa, el abismo horrible y el nocturno
opaco, que nunca se desvía aunque
los hombres han construido tantos puentes
patriarcas encima de la marea y el
arroyo, sobre la ola, sobre el hoyo.
Usted nos mira y usted
se arrima a nosotros despacio, poco
a poco con movimientos de un ave
terrenal, y oye un fragmento, fragmento
de verso, como un trozo de un bolero
pero una canción sin guitarra o cuatro,
sin melodía, unos fragmentos rotos
literalmente de las planas claras,
oye cuando traspasan el vidrio que
aparta mas que contiene este libro y
detiene en su ser un mundo más de su
visión de su ser, trasoye algo breve
entre las vocales 'a' y 'o'. Y usted se halla a
sí mismo en la cama en la noche oscura
y tiene los ojos abiertos pero
se ve nada, literalmente nada,

y puede imaginarse sin límite en
cualquier parte siquiera ahí donde los
sentidos humanos no pueden mostrar
lo contrario, una liberación pura,
y recuerda la música de voces
y la temperatura de una piel en
la plena luz del sol, más o menos al
mediodía, móviles. Sabe que este es
el amor, nadie puede decir más o
explicar lo que ocurre en su ser: amor
es una palabra de dos sílabas
está hablado en dos voces en seguida
en planos invisibles pero claros,
móvil y con alta temperatura.

SEXO

El alfabeto del sexo emprende equis
y que esa x es la primera letra,
la escritura manifiesta así lo que es:
los enloquecidos símbolos se creen
criaturas vivas aunque no lo sean,
se hacen genitales, se hacen figuras.
La vagina deletrea con x
«exacto es el son de la venadita,
benditos sean todos los animales
que con genitales están escritos»
deletreada con X.
La verga es otra cosa, analfabeta,
letrada en la equis de unas mil penas:
pieles blancas enviadas como cartas
postales, o correo electrónico,
cuya ontología tan dudosa está.
California es el sitio sexual, frío,
y mentiras son las otras historias
contadas por unas líneas celosas,
tan lejos de noche y la red de nada
que algo sexual no tiene una pareja.
La ciudad, Los Angeles,
Este lado cogiendo descuidado,
los cuerpos de las letras se desbordan,
equis vaginas con rayas borradas,
borrachas con rayas las vergas X.
Desconocido pueblo de las horas
de los días de las pieles ocultas,
visibles momentos en ecos de pies
actuales en los caracteres negros,

en los textos carnales anónimos,
conocidos, y ellos bien deletreados,
porque equis comienza el acto del sexo,
germina la cadena de las letras
en ambas la verga y la vagina
de Los Angeles, ahí en el lado Este.
El sexo aquí articula
tan noche el lado este, tan bestial, penal,
se penetra el acto de sentido ante
el animalado acto de hacer letras:
la equis no vale no más ni por su alma
y se convierte en símbolos bestiales;
de las dos líneas, una permanece
virginal como un pinto deshuevado,
pero al otro lado, la otra línea no
simula lo que fue, un más manso perro,
sorpresa, en cambio, la otra se deslía,
línea, como monja desarreglada,
se derrama del orden de la raya:
línea se convierte en letras, C y S.
¿Cómo se escribe el sexo?
Sé ese modo de animar, como animan
los animales alfabetizados,
C línea S, verga cruza vagina,
rosa raya aguacate, equis ausente.
Cruzada, sin preferencia, la gata
negra no halla en la muerte ni en la raya
C y S ni una diferencia oculta,
ni misterio ante la letra o la otra:
negra es la noche negra,
negra la falda de la noche negra,
también sombra en la isla nocturna, sombra,
negro aire de piel nocturna, rayada,

gris tras negro tras gris tras negro tras gris,
equis línea sexo, equis C y S,
tras la negra faja de la noche tras
el movimiento de la negra gata
que es la danza sexual de la estampa equis,
que es el ánima de la huella C y S:
Sí, las cruces emprenden el sexo aquí,
el acto nos hace y nos hace al revés,
el equis gato es la gatita negra,
sombras gruesas y caracteres negros
en las blancas sábanas y brillantes
caminantes que cruzan la calle ancha
antojándose la negra letra equis.

Muerte

Hágase el corazón una inglaterra:
ínsula, pequeña, baja. Hágase
cambiar el ritmo: deje atrás el pulso;
goce una lluvia débil, incesante,
y baje todas las temperaturas,
incluyendo grados y pulmonías
de los poetas románticos, cada una.
Hágase el corazón un imperio, sí
con heráldica, herederos y herencia,
con una línea real, verde y húmeda,
honrosa aunque asquerosa. La bandera
debe estar verde y mojado todo hasta
la chispa. La música también debe
sembrar las lágrimas de vez en cuando.
Olvídese de las penas porque aquí
todo es lo mismo: estará cansado
al despertar tal como al subir pisos.
Además, los libros cuestan bastante
y los autores escriben bastantes
versos. No dura mucho tiempo para
aprender a tomar café mudado,
café de hierba fresca y fragante, y no más
estará un poco más difícil para
entender las reglas de las fragancias,
y todo huele bastante. La reina
no será su amiga, no se lo olvide,

le tratará de irlandés, pero puede
declamar unas escenas teatrales
ella sin equivocación, ¡que viva!
Hágase el cuerpo un papel. Cada día
escríbame algo triste y mándeme la
voluntad por las manos o el vello de
la mejilla. No se olvide de traer
lápices, las computadoras están
superfluas, acuérdese. Verdes, las
corrientes corren hasta los fines de
la insulita: corra también hasta tal
filo. Hágase el corazón ladrillo,
hinque la rodilla a la hora de albañil.

Love in the Time
of Aftershocks

6.7

I   ABSENCE, THE FIRST INSTANCE

Loss, as in love, the pause, respite, moment of interval
between breaths, inhale, exhale, the moment of pause: think for
a moment, is the stop at lung's fill or lack? Yes, the pause in the
rhythm of motion of air, a life, one could imagine, in the in
between of air motion, and the wait, of very being, the wait of
air, the supporting ether of flight, the wait of wings, diaphanous
angels, the breath of wings of that stop that enables the rhyme
of flight, the wings of angels: Stopped, just then, we are sure,
we are all sure, city of angels, of wings and breaths, and air
moving, flight suspended, just then, an interval of the silent and
sure of the very breath of the angels, of the city of my birth, the
city that infused me life that wrote me *in spiritus*, just then, in
the in between of my very breath, moment mine, interval I
breathe between just then. It is like that space between beats:
within the gap of systole and diastole, of heart like drum,
between the down and the up of beat, just then, caught in
arrest, mid beat, unsure of the dance, of the very rhythm itself
mid flight. So it is as it seems if sight is an arrow and the city of
angels lags from its flight, it is just so: wait a motion and it has
passed, silent and slight air, see it is so, city mine. Just then in
the pause and in the empty break, arbiter of difference, in the
lag and gap and stop mid flow: it is as it seems, mid flight amid
the flap of wings of angels in flight in the city at night. So it
means this and this is what is seen if what just then is taken for
real, if the blank of the clock while we inhale or ex is taken as
time, as the moment to which it refers, and thus we mean what
we separate: this from that, in from out, flight from night,
diaphanous flight of mine. Night and the absence of night as its
negative, black and the absence of blank as its clone, and time
in shard we cannot gather nor hold but watch pierce our palms

in the shade mid day, just then but at night in the city of flight
and the flight angelic of the city of night and pause and silent
flow of light air like so much breath of the dead, the angelic,
the holy, all in so much faint air motion beatified, just then and
it is not, it is gone, if that can be a present, a gift of time, as in
the impossible moment we note just then in the night city
between the halves of the beat that rewrites our being in so
significant and so real movements of life making, as in a pause
to sigh and finding meaning in its envisioning. So? It is so, for
it can be no other way if to be other is denied strictly on
temporal non parallelism grounds like the way space is so
cleverly impossible to afford the ambiguous, one means what
one is, facilely and blind like. It is not precisely because it is:
city of angel night, in flight solo.

II THE INEFFICIENCY OF SLEEP

Off Beverly Blvd the sense of one woman alone in sleep as
if an art, a script of death perhaps, for this is Hollywood and
love is all it seems in an act or two, the sense not unlike absence
but not that final awe, rather more the innocent murder of
hearts, one in line after the next, fresh blood in the sense of
solitude and the alone of the mammal in hunt: so silent in
tracks across snow if there ever would be such in this city, this
place of such sense, where image and sleep conflict in the light
of day, in the contact with spoken Spanish on the broad streets
and the traffic of humans waiting change for some better, a
solitude, cruel in its purity, simplicity, and its fine atonement
like sacrament by script and brief and fleeting sight: but such is
the hard solitude of the image as commodity and the shadow it
tracks across the snow, if such could be, of the emotional city's
range. She knows 6.7 as the imprint in the space of her heart,
beneath an indifferent breast left and pale nipple, there in the
inner enclave there is nothing left that can be imagined by any
string of practiced words, nothing of so severe a number, one
that so cuts the organs of emotion, nothing like absence, like
patch over well, so buried in the lack that can be imagined by
the single foe in the sharp guise of the lover, subject to the
unwanted arrow of desire, to wide eros, and the blatant and
stupid move, so like so much unseen dumb air. 6.7 marks her,
scent like, beneath the gloss of skin in the light of camera and
the DNA house that breathes and beats her into existence at
every instant: but if we can imagine, can extrapolate the shard
of instant, the interval between the beats of life, into a stretched
and extended span, from mid beat to slice of day, night actually,
of sleep in solitude, then such number and such genetic code
mark her, her personal scent of chosen fragrance and secret

body, then mark in the night of solitary sleeping, alone and unwilling to utter anything other than no in the course of so solitary a sleep: this is the trick of Hollywood: there is nothing beneath the gloss because it truly cannot control time except by illusion, where it lives and words, so the gloss is the meaning, the string of words are to be executed and nothing more, at the cessation of lights, all go home, but there is no home, just place, just one then for solitary sleep, for sleeping alone like a film can beside so many others or not, but self contained and hermetic, with a cleanliness born of its sad inefficiency: so alone it need invent language at every instant if it is to confirm its solitary self, unable in the loneliness of the dumb sleep to reach to the lover as subject of words and words as subject of language itself as a shared medium. Thus the inefficiency of it all. It is so much easier to hurt alone, to fling arrows to true targets and to sleep dumb and refuse to have to make up words at every instant, than to hold one other: this is the lesson of a city so born in the image of video, in motion represented by magnetic particle arrangements on long ribbons of place. No is the only carry over in the scene of the solitary and absent, so there is no recourse for the sad angel's breast left exposed, a pre-perspective painting, the verso of icon. An inefficient sleep follows inefficient sleep and solitude accumulates like so many leavings or wrinkles of sad age or lessons of life learned and unlearned because we live in time, such a sad inefficient opportunity left blank, a moment of nothing perfected to a lifestyle performed for the dream of a camera obscura that follows after the lights have ceased and the crew gone, imagined to carry over to the sleep of the real, from the imagined reel, to the performance of solitary sleep: what position? what fare? what dumb show?

III   Cognizance

The sense of motion is natural, as if truth, our skins, membranes that withhold our fluid bodies from an exterior of aridity, of spill, of infection, of change as desiccation or decomposition or at the least from what we enjoy. But the attendant sense of dislocation defies the law of the single whole, when played out a here is never again except as a permanence of *there* or a so fleeting *near here* as to incite wonder. And so he wakes, first of all wet, covered in the sweats of the impervious image, recalling and calling to her as if she could share the space in the now. Wakes clear headed sure of the failure of the imaging sense, fully sure of how its meaning tracks without fear as if in hunt of some vital organ for transplant and transport to the first world country, in that manner she causes the sensation of waking just then as the trace of the faint trail, cold now as it has been for so long, nevertheless incites the hunter in that logical convolution where the hunter identifies and then becomes the one hunted: at this point it happens; this, the lesson: a number is so much, it cannot paint absence. Because space is always space between, being nothing without definition, an edge, boundaries, that act always confirms state. The *of what* remains a question in the deep dark of morning before the sun and before any hint of natural life, the *of what* that is cause, even in momentary oscillation from the effect, that is truly the object and subject of the physical articulation, like perspiration just then, the question so like a *the* after sensing an echo, physically imprinted momentarily on the auditory organ, beyond the actual hearing, after the spent sound, but the plain physical affect of its former presence. And just as easily the what slides into who, even if resisting a bit the further slide to whom, and the question evolves from the abject site of distant truth to the palpable matter of a skin, a scent of hair, a flash of color shot by a breeze or shake of head: the images awaken sharp like any but the most devastating earthquakes, as if 'beyond image,' as the French say, like her touch for real. For who is one body. In that sharp shake awake, the slap of light from so lost a deep darkness, she in image brings him into cognizance as if into being itself, the who so importantly effecting a whom into a who in a play of subject and object and the dance of light and scent. So what was prior, in the dreamless sleep in the absent light, in the black womb that does not exist beyond simple myth, in the dead of time itself? Dead as in rock, glass, clock, tide. Wake as in beyond death, a ritual perhaps.

IV THE PRESENT

Take life as a gift. To possess it at the present moment in
the city of the angels is better than any other she could quickly
name off hand. In City Terrace at this very moment there are
birds making sound; they flit from perch in the tall bush and
hedge amid petals the color of flushed skin, some wine, and the
rare cut of ripe nectarine. This she knows will never pass again
and she is witness to a singularity: it is enough to surpass the
need for sex, enough in a true way, so die just then and have
fully realized the stuff of living, completely. So she inhales just
then like no other human ever has and holds for a split
powerful atoms of air, the very keys to life, and peers out the
curved window in Lomas, terrace to the city of angels. It is a
gift she gives herself: she knows and touches her forearm with
three fingers of her left hand, slow, in the manner that would
excite him, so simple, were he here and awake, both at the same
time, this once. To touch oneself is so much more than plane
confirmation, it is, rather, the impossibility of the gift, at once
inconsequential and of great consequence. She exhales and
disperses that particular peace of air, having tasted its use,
having made it function, and having done so, sent it to plant, to
tree most of all she hopes. To imagine ends because of simple
transition is plain logic she knows, poor in its waste and wide in
its aim, and therefore resists the definition of origin and of end,
rejects etiology as a disease in itself. She takes light and warms,
breathes and hears birds who use air like stair, like slide, like
piece of thing, and grateful for the present precisely because it
incarnates undefined by an imaginary what was and an
oppressive will be. "City Terrace." And just as easily it is a fear,
loose and without referent, no cause in its present wrappings,
just as easily a fear like heights or open spaces or some strange

insect: she is after all in so dry a place on the planet, rain it seems is never more than a memory which is a dream which is a lie which is dead anyway. Before she reaches her near wrist, she finds wonder in an apprehension, so silent, colorless and pale, very unlike skin, more like air in cough and draft: it is a fear and a means to fear, boundless in its awe on an unbordered field of play dislocated like flight. Just then. Lomas is the negation of the valley and all. In the undulations of surface taken for still in the moment of present, as present, fluctuations in space, so that up and down simultaneously are beside one another: that is Lomas, sheets of curved space, a surface that fights you and holds you and sets you up, she knows, like the valley but its negation, in affirmation of sky instead of the valley's emulation of hell and tectonic underpinnings, the *semper obscura* of the beneath and core. Simple, she believes in her simple act of taking in air and expelling air in rhythm she is making life in a progressive tense, in an idealization of invisible air, a palpable, sensible body of body. If fear is a gift in time, dead time, across a still undulation of curved space, and if too, an affirmation of ritual as in the dance of the olfactory when confronting the magic of flight, then the gift of life holds out the promise of affirmation as so much petal of color before a casual stop of bird: not more, as in the spill of hours and the desiccation of them as well, some aloe scent trick. She hears the sounds of birds, close to perceiving the birds themselves. Birds, air, petals, skin, alive in the present of the gift.

V   What Is Taken in Sex

Streets do meet, for example the boulevards Santa Monica and Wilshire or Santa Monica and Sunset meet and cross in different zones in the site of the angels. Do on the Westside, a site of diasporic New York and do on the other, a Sunset of Spanish, stubborn resistance to bear flags and grizzly extinction. People do too. The clearest metaphor is sex in its sense of the act, motion and conflation, and in its sense of procreation, as the killing of death and stifling hour. Near the cross of Sunset and Santa Monica, in Echo Park and in Silverlake, two people wait in separate houses simultaneously thinking of each other at the same time wondering if procreation had begun at recent coupling, in the exchange of body scent and the pressure and motion of intimate touch. It was five days after the Santa Monica freeway collapse at La Cienega beside the Kaiser Hospital where each, unknown to the other, took plus and minus tests in the modern fear from intimacy that scores so much contemporary energy. But sex as a metaphor is a weak lie. At best. For to envision anything that is not sex as sex is the so transparent a strategy as to delight no one except practitioners of psychology and religion. It is rather, as in is, as cuts sense or contacts meaning or best of all abuts connection, a metonym. His house in Echo Park, half way between the lake and Alvarado, up a poor hill, is in a profound sense an intermediary link between his body and the violent number of just a week past, that is, house as metonym for him and for the earthquake. But in the sharp and sudden and over before it is conceived essence of the large number, there is the echo's tale that lingers, that is nothing in that it is not, but that inspires meaning for the five days later aftershock, so well timed in the act of sex, the very act that might signal his procreation if waiting so proves.

House tying self and tectonic shift in metonymy, which otherwise might be construed as metaphor of himself and the earthquake or worst, of orgasm and the earth shake into a natural orgasm. Hers is in Silverlake near a park, creased beside another hill, close as bird, connected by Sunset as boulevard and as transitory view of magenta smog display from respective front, flat windows at each birth of night across the city of night. Her name is monosyllabic, consonantal, a fact that fought her blind until she moved to the locus of epicenters beside the far coast, and for the first time in a city of vowels, appended her name and acquired an unexpected measure of peace. Which now in the expectation of shock is a diminished peace, one scratched and worn, insufficient to the demands of life in the present. Coupled at the instant five days after the 6.7 in a violent heave of ground and groan, cry, of her house walls, windows, and stuff, she grabbed for him to pull him even closer than sex can unite two, and dug her nails and pulled eight tracks of scratch across his insensate back, almost as if to recount and arouse the matter of fear itself. It is the period of wait that the ether pervades, the heavy pressure measured in atmospheres of the period of wait, in tension, apprehension, desire and anxiety. Her house is redolent with passion, everywhere signs of activity: long cracks emerge from nowhere on walls and dive toward joints, there must still be sharp bits of glass everywhere, from mirror and glass and the sole deco cat that crashed, invisible and heckling shards recanting. And beyond semen, it is perhaps the ubiquity of fertilization itself that so writes each room with the smell of skin and the narration how people are made. After so telling a tectonic clash, other shocks will follow; of this there can be no doubt: she knows and waits and crosses days off calendars as if numbers meant anything more than a fabrication by men to underwrite pain. So they measure distance: he from Echo Park to a womb in doubt, she from Silverlake to a genital of liquid, from aural retort to shards of yet indeterminant weight. Metonym is measured from metonym in a mediation of pretense, in a pregnant span of something both spatial and temporal, kinesis and spiritus, man as fluid, woman as fluid. It is an unbearable wait, without end because so pervasive even as to cut sleep, like adulterated drug, impure and fooling only those who desire. So much in number as if number were life, so much in sequence, in order, in link and line: an aftershock is like an echo, awaited, but a new quake again, like a human born, a period of heavy wait in a present of perpetual acuity, awake in apprehension even in sleep, counting off so many dead numbers, life consequence chaos.

VI ACTING SEX

In this city, sex followed the automobile; it was an, albeit necessary, afterthought. Orgasm here is literally the consequence of a sex drive. In the time of aftershocks nothing stops: that the Santa Monica freeway is down stops no one: people fuck in vans defiantly flaunt before angels in awesome free flight. One couple does from Atlantic Blvd down Whittier Blvd, Sixth Street, Wilshire, and Santa Monica, in a rough straight line to the Pacific Coast Highway and the ocean itself: in an act of ritual creation from ocean to ocean. They recognize their small human irony—he, from the Pacific edge of the continent lives just off Atlantic Blvd, and she, from the right coast, lives in Venice, just off the Pacific. They drive holding each other's genitals like keys to the wonder of the times, and in motion at Main and Hill, they capture the aftershock: something is confirmed: at the very least a statement of existence, at the most, a deification. For this couple consumption must always follow copulation and find the greatest distance from his ancestral cuisine and hers in a simulacrum of Africa, just blocks from the aftershock. Their economy is simple: friction requires fructose.

VII SEX AMONG THE DEAD

Acts and is late (than capitalism, or postmodernism), and
before asks, he recalls the lyric and fashions the request to
"crash" at her place rather than, being "in no shape for
driving," return to San Fernando; they could tomorrow find
together Ritchie Valens's grave and visit the adobe mission all as
they stop by his place to gather his stuff, and maybe, if the bent
for morbidity and vacuous voyeur leaves her, check out Cal
State Northridge, to bear witness to almost 7 with all senses
turned up full. Her place in Whittier is her place, marked so by
a crisscrossing across every square foot, by small regular print
on long sheets of paper, by menageries of things, the origin of
each of which she could recite like water, and by the mantle of
confidence she takes on within its confines: fence, street, hedge,
walls, particular light, familiar procession of clouds pausing en
route to La Puente. Of course it is no, but there is no rush for
each such occasion affords the opportunity to perform, and it is
the delivery that, after all, is what truly communicates: there is
no and there is no, and neither can touch the other in shimmer,
sheen or affect. This could be and so is the occasion to
extrapolate, not only could he not stay, but, why not, their trip
to Ensenada was off. So in the wait for timing in the formation
of posture, nature interrupts with an aftershock, it being after
all, January 22 exactly pm, and it is an event and a moment,
expected in hard anticipation for this is the term of aftershocks:
an interim of sensory arousal, a reason for sexual acts, for the
rite of remaking the human race, for making life in a physical
way from the writhing moans and sudden shaking of two
coupled as if outside time, "beyond being" as the Russians say,
or "beyond life" as the Québecoise poet bemoaned a life
truncated all too soon, absence as the telos of cold a juncture

among three rivers. But *no* is an affirmation taking loose time and slapping an order to dis the shaking earth, a move bearable only on solid ground, far from the bleeding tectonics, where lack of motion gives birth to both flippant and careless abandon and unbearable levity that is otherwise meted out fluidly between two people engaged in sex and born on the rim, tentatively. That is in a move that bases its trajectory on absolute mass and a firmness of spirit, one that can therefore assume action as if on a flat and immobile place where the dance of the self is all that truly orchestrates any meaning from the solitary motion in the still and near dead site. Or stage, if you will, as in transitory feat, locating realization in daily increment, a stage for working out the hectic pace and consequent effects of being, where on stage supersedes at in the fact of self articulation, as that born of stone and bedrock where negation is a proprietary impulse as much as the reel limits of stage, her stage, as in state of being, no, in the here, no. The act of agency, the agent's act, just at the actor's agent, delimiting the walls of hours of potential within the confines of so lighted a state and stage of being: in the bright light and systole/diastole music of any auditor's ah, any moment of pure reception, taken from the actor as pure light, transparent truth, and negation of blurring of lines. No, nothing in any country. No, never.

VIII INSTANCE, THE FIRST LOSS

This then is the some of the moments collected involuntarily
in frantic instances of wide sensory receptivity: the recollection
of a cruise down Whittier Blvd may be broken into image pieces
of sensory data, of sense of youth, of the only gloss of Tudi's
pearl white, 13 coat lacquer off the long and at times dancing
hood, may be so in a defiant rush to individuate and to, by the
law of opposites, the trick of irony, valorize what it ostensibly
occludes, that is, offer flash of scene and sense in a disguise
masquerade decoy cover from the awful fact of order and that of
unforgiving sequence. There is the sense that any drive down
Whittier, regardless how imagined, must in reality proceed
according to fashion, which is after all an order, that posits, as
base structure, that motion must have direction, sequence, and
singular occupation of transitory space. The recollection of
broken sensations, of images tossed vividly, is so much a lie, one
constructed to imbue subject matter, that is, to locate a fleeting
present, with meaning, tautologically meaningful because it is
so, and further a lie because the comfort of the truth is a well
sealed casket in black peat and damp. For at base, the cruise
down Whittier is as governed a flight across the Santa Monica
to the San Diego at night after sex, as cast as left turn from Hill
onto Main admiring the huge glass windows of the cafe, as the
sequence from first, in a non-numerical sense, to second and
on to last. In truth the infinity from zero to one is never
transversed because we are never allotted nothing zero, never
face the awful lacuna and lake of difference, but are set so
deceptively in motion from the first swimming of crazed sperm
and the slow dance of proud ovum: and in this simple sequence
of events, it is the truth and reality of the unavoidable sequence
of event-ness that we may try to obfuscate with color and rhyme

and the trick of art, psychosis, orgasm, fear, love. This is the awful lesson and state of being of the instances of the aftershocks: 6.7 is done, written into memory like fire so abruptly that we could observe the finality of everything, but done nonetheless, but the months agonize afterwards, agon, and we live alive heightened to defy what is to follow: and what is to follow is a truth and a reality we have no business to restrict, for it ignores our significance so much like a wounded god or aborting goddess. We can defy precisely because of insignificance, small waves or particles, of density and length too small to effect. And so we prescribe the only trick that works, the act that makes humans, the act that sets up the impossible synchronization of two bodies in motion, that writes as subject the stuff that is the very line itself; an act so sacred it is abandon itself. After 6.7 at the site of angels, in the city of night, sex is an act of defiant passion, a moment of intensity that unwrites the instance-ness of raw sensing nerve endings, rewrites act itself with agency and a drive toward the sea. In the Time of Aftershocks, love is the sex of the act, is the act performed in the sight of the angels, defiant before the gods, before nature, coupling in the city of night, in the bare and awful span.